Snowy Owl Invasion!

Tracking an Unusual Migration

SANDRA MARKLE

MILLBROOK PRESS / MINNEAPOLIS

For dear friends Lance and Sarah Wiegand and their children:
Alexander, Benjamin, Catherine, Davis, Elizabeth, and Fairyn

The author would like to thank the following people for sharing their enthusiasm and expertise: Dr. David Brinker, wildlife biologist and cofounder of Project SNOWstorm; Dr. Denver Holt, President of the Owl Research Institute; Steve Huy, naturalist; Ken Knowles, naturalist and birder tour leader for Wildland Tours, Newfoundland, Canada; Andrew J. McGann, Product Specialist, Cellular Tracking Technologies, LLC; Norman Smith, Director of Mass Audubon's Society Blue Hills Trailside Museum, Milton, Massachusetts; and Scott Weidensaul, Founding Board Member of the Ned Smith Center for Nature and Art, Millersburg, Pennsylvania, and cofounder of Project SNOWstorm. A special thank-you to Skip Jeffery for his loving support during the creative process.

Millbrook Press™
An imprint of Lerner Publishing
241 First Avenue North
Minneapolis, MN 55401 USA

For reading levels and more information, look up this title at www.lernerbooks.com.

Main body text set in Caecilia Com. Typeface provided by Linotype AG.

Library of Congress Cataloging-in-Publication Data

Names: Markle, Sandra, author.
Title: Snowy owl invasion! : tracking an unusual migration / by Sandra Markle.
Description: Minneapolis : Millbrook Press, [2018] | Audience: Ages 8–12. | Audience: Grades 4 to 6. | Includes bibliographical references and index. Identifiers: LCCN 2017010741 (print) | LCCN 2017030113 (ebook) | ISBN 9781512498653 (eb pdf) | ISBN 9781512431063 (lb : alk. paper)
Subjects: LCSH: Snowy owl—Behavior—Juvenile literature. | Snowy owl—Migration—Juvenile literature. | Animal migration—Juvenile literature.
Classification: LCC QL696.S83 (ebook) | LCC QL696.S83 M3225 2018 (print) | DDC 598.9/7—dc23

LC record available at https://lccn.loc.gov/2017010741

Manufactured in the United States of America
3-52433-23516-2/28/2022

CONTENTS

THE INVASION

On a cold, windy day in November 2013, wildlife biologist David Brinker trudged across Assateague Island in Maryland. He was searching for saw-whet owls as part of a project to study their migration (travels north and south). But what he found instead surprised him. On one sand dune, peeking through winter-dried plants, sat a big white bird—*a snowy owl.*

Snowy owls often rest on the ground and are naturally colored to blend in.

These big owls spend summers hunting and breeding in the Arctic. Most remain in the Arctic year-round. However, each winter some migrate south to have less competition for food. It was unusual to see any as far south as Maryland, though. Yet this was the second snowy owl Brinker had seen on Assateague in the past couple of weeks.

Over the next week, Brinker noticed that bird-watchers online were reporting an unusual number of snowy owl sightings in Canada. The reports from the Cape Race area, at the southeastern tip of Newfoundland, Canada, were amazing: 43 snowy owls, or snowies, spotted on November 23; 138 on December 1; and 206 on December 8. According to Ken Knowles, a birding tour leader in that area, "It's rare to see more than ten snowy owls in an entire winter. Within this short time, I saw more than I'd seen in thirty years."

Brinker was fascinated. "Clearly, this year snowies were pouring south out of the Arctic," he said. "Something *big* was going on."

So what was it?

Snowy owls traveled south and stayed for the winter—even in Washington, DC.

HISTORY IN THE MAKING

In the Arctic, snowy owls usually keep to themselves except during the breeding season.

Scientists call what happened during the 2013–2014 winter an irruption. That's a sudden population increase of an animal in an area where it's not usually found. In an irruption, migrating animals often invade areas far beyond their normal range, such as Arctic snowies traveling in large numbers to parts of southern Canada and the United States.

What causes an irruption of snowy owls? Why were there so many snowies along the Atlantic coast that winter? The answer has to do with the previous summer and why there were so many snowies that year.

The female (*right*) is eating a lemming delivered by the male (*left*). He supplies food while she alone stays on their nest, keeping the eggs warm while the chicks inside develop.

Every summer in the Arctic, mature snowy owls—adults at least three years old and older—pair up and mate. The more well fed the female is, the more eggs she lays. In a good year, females are likely to produce six to eight eggs. But in 2013, scientists studying snowy owls found nests with as many as ten or eleven eggs.

To be healthy, produce eggs, and hatch chicks, a female snowy owl needs to eat five to seven adult-sized lemmings every day.

After laying her eggs, the female stays on the nest to incubate them for about a month. Meanwhile, the male hunts to supply her with food. For snowies, that's mainly lemmings—hamster-sized rodents (relatives of rats and mice). Once the chicks hatch, the male must catch and deliver even more food so the female can feed their family.

At first, chicks have a thick downy coat to keep them warm—even their feet are covered (*left*). Chicks grow bigger fast. But it takes about another forty-five to fifty-five days for them to shed their downy coat and develop feathers (*right*).

The female snowy owl stays on the nest for about another three weeks. She keeps the chicks warm while their downy coats grow fluffy and thick. She also guards them from other hunters, such as arctic foxes.

At first, she tears up food for the chicks. But within a few weeks, the chicks are kitten-sized and they can gulp down whole lemmings. They need to eat a lot to grow and fledge (develop wing muscles and flight feathers) so they can fly. In 2013 getting enough to eat wasn't an issue—there was more than enough food for healthy mothers and growing chicks. The snowy owl population boomed that year thanks to a lemming population explosion.

Owl breeding behavior expert Denver Holt reported seeing as many as thirty lemmings at once scattered around a nest, killed and dropped there by a father snowy. This was chick food waiting to be eaten. No wonder so many of the chicks that hatched during the 2013 summer survived to become healthy, young adults by winter. Holt said, "Lemmings drive the whole Arctic ecosystem."

And as winter arrived, the booming population of snowy owls spread beyond the Arctic as well. Snowy population swells often result in irruptions, as competition for hunting territories pushes owls south. Indeed, that year would be a remarkable example.

The chicks stay in the nest until they are about three weeks old. Then they wander to hide from predators such as foxes. During this time, the parents keep track of where the chicks go and bring them food.

LOTS OF LEMMINGS

If the huge snowy owl population came about because of the lemmings, what caused the lemming population to boom? In fact, their population cycles over time. Reports show big increases about every four years. It all depends on certain conditions being just right.

A large population starts with spring and summer conditions favoring plants, such as grasses and sedges, that produce lots of seeds—lemming food. Then, in the winter, lemmings need the ground not to ice over so they can dig down and reach seeds that plants dropped in the summer and fall. And they need good quality snow cover.

That means they need the snow to form a thick blanket, shielding them from the cold air as they

Lemmings have fat, round bodies with short legs, little flat ears, and only a nub of a tail—perfect for holding onto body heat in their cold home environment.

scurry through the tunnels they dig. But the snow also has to be fluffy enough to trap air for them to breathe and soft enough to make tunneling easy. Then males and females can continue to find each other, mate, and produce young all winter long.

Lemmings can begin mating when they're just three weeks old. Babies need only about a month to develop, and a mother gives birth to a litter of three to seven babies—sometimes even more when there is plenty of food. If conditions are right, she'll have up to four litters per year.

"Where ideal climate conditions do exist," said Holt, "once the snow melts in the spring, there's an insane number of lemmings."

Whenever they can, lemmings tunnel through soil or snow to avoid predators while they search for food.

SNOWIES BECOME SNOWBIRDS

Snowy owls are naturally dressed for winter weather. They have a double coat of densely packed feathers, even over their legs and around their beak.

The snowy owl irruption of 2013–2014 was historic not only because so many owls migrated from their summer home but also because they traveled so much farther south than usual, through Canada and deep into the United States. Snowies spread beyond the types of wild areas they normally prefer. People spotted these owls sitting on fences at airports, on houses, on cars, on city park benches—and even on window ledges of skyscrapers.

A snowy owl in Washington, DC

SPOTTING SNOWY

For most people, seeing a wild snowy owl is a rare treat. Snowy owls are among the largest owl species (types of living things). An adult snowy is about 20 inches (52 cm) long from the top of its head to the tip of its tail feathers. Its wingspan, the distance between the tips of its outstretched wings, is typically just over 4 feet (1.2 m). And it weighs about 4.5 pounds (2 kg), about the same as half a gallon (1.9 L) of milk.

But if you spot a snowy owl, how can you tell whether you've seen a male or a female? If two or more birds are together, the bigger owl is likely a female. Females also usually have more heavily barred patterns (horizontal, colored bands) on their feathers throughout their lives.

Look closely at this male (*left*) and female (*right*) snowy owl pair. What are all the ways the male snowy looks different from the female?

Snowy owls fly with powerful downstrokes, quick upstrokes, and short glides.

Young males are also likely to have barred patterns, while older males are usually paler and may be snowy white.

While you can't tell the age of an older snowy, you can tell if a snowy owl just hatched the previous summer. Snowies molt (shed and replace) all of their body feathers annually. But each year, they molt only a few of the long feathers at the edges of their wings, the feathers that control their flight. So a snowy owl has a set of completely shiny, brightly barred wing feathers only for the year it fledges.

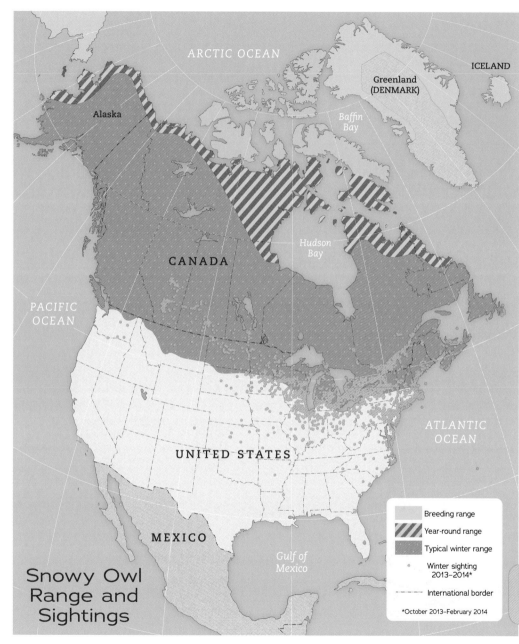

ARCTIC OCEAN

ICELAND

Greenland
(DENMARK)

Alaska

Baffin
Bay

CANADA

Hudson
Bay

PACIFIC
OCEAN

ATLANTIC
OCEAN

UNITED STATES

MEXICO

Gulf of
Mexico

Snowy Owl
Range and
Sightings

Breeding range

Year-round range

Typical winter range

Winter sighting
2013–2014*

International border

*October 2013–February 2014

During the winter irruption of 2013–2014, people recorded 1,117 snowy owl sightings. That was the most snowy owl sightings since 1926–1927, when there were 2,363 sightings reported—nearly all from the northeastern United States. During the irruption of 2013–2014, while the majority of snowy owls were spotted in the Northeast and around the Great Lakes, people also recorded sightings in the South. According to reports, that year snowies traveled all the way to Kentucky, Georgia, and as far south as Florida.

Look closely at this map. Did any snowies travel to where you live during the irruption?

Scientists aren't sure why so many snowy owls headed south out of the Arctic during the 2013–2014 winter, but they have a number of ideas. One possibility ties in with the unusually large number of snowies that hatched and survived to become young adults in 2013. Because of this, there was more competition than normal among snowy owls to claim hunting territories on the Arctic tundra. Snowies normally fight one another and also compete with other wintertime hunters, such as arctic foxes. But experts think that during the 2013–2014 winter, there may have been so much competition that lots of snowies were pushed farther south, away from the Arctic tundra.

Arctic foxes are about the size of an average adult house cat. So you can see that adult snowies are big owls. And it's no wonder they compete with arctic foxes for the same prey—this time a scrap of musk ox.

WHAT IS TUNDRA?

Tundra is the coldest of all the environments where animals and plants live. It is the environment found in the Arctic, Antarctic, and high up on mountains, such as the Alps and the Himalayas. Tundra areas have a short growing season for plants and very little rainfall. Most of the available water comes from the surface snowmelt. A shallow layer of soil under the snow also thaws. However, beneath that is permafrost (permanently frozen ground).

With their feathered coats of white or white and brown, snowies are outfitted to stay warm and perfectly disguised to blend in and hunt in this often snow-covered environment.

The growing season for plants on the Arctic tundra is only about two months long.

Strong winds are another possible reason the young snowies headed south. That year heavy winds often blew from the northwest toward the southeast. As snowies flew in search of winter hunting territories to claim, these winds might have launched the birds away from the tundra, over forests. This would have been an unfamiliar landscape. So perhaps the snowies kept on flying in search of tundra.

Many snowies didn't stop until they reached big open fields, the shores of the Great Lakes, or Canadian and northeastern US coasts, areas that may have seemed like tundra to them. For owls that arrived later, competition with those already settled in those places might have pushed them even farther south.

For the snowies, the forests were a totally different environment from the tundra landscape.

GOOD NEWS, BAD NEWS

At their winter destinations, Arctic snowy owls found a nice reward—a wide range of food options. Some snowies hunted ducks and other waterbirds, including medium-sized geese. Other snowies hunted rabbits, rats, muskrats, and meadow voles (a rodent similar to lemmings). The young birds were still learning to hunt, but having so much prey available meant they had more chances to catch a meal.

This snowy owl is carrying a meal of duck to the shelter of a resting spot away from other snowies.

A SNOWY'S DINNER

For a snowy owl, the goal of the day—every day—is to eat its fill without using up a lot of energy. A snowy owl perches and waits until it sees prey to launch its attack. Then it takes flight, moving at speeds up to 50 miles (80 km) per hour. It uses its sharp talons to kill. It tears up big prey with its beak and swallows it in chunks. Smaller prey is swallowed whole—headfirst, in one gulp.

A snowy owl has no teeth, but it doesn't need to chew. The bird's digestive juices and internal muscle action break down the soft parts of what it eats. Hard bits, such as bones and feathers, are filtered out in the bird's gizzard. These pack together into a pellet that is pushed up and out of its mouth.

The pellet partly blocks the owl's digestive system so it has to push out the pellet to hunt and eat again.

Of course, the owls still faced competition for their food. Although lots of prey was available during the 2013–2014 irruption, lots of snowies had traveled south. So they competed with one another for the best hunting spots, such as where they could grab ducks from a group settled to sleep on a lake at night.

During the irruption, scientists reported snowies were willing to share resting places while they slept. Awake, bigger snowies were likely to attack smaller owls.

Another result of the large irruption was bad news for both people and the owls. While competing for hunting territories in urban areas, many snowies were drawn to airports. It's likely these flat open places reminded them of their tundra home. But airport visits were dangerous for both owls and people. If the birds landed on a runway, they could interfere with a plane's takeoff or landing.

So airports worked with local organizations to remove the owls. Norman Smith, director of the Mass Audubon's Blue Hills Trailside Museum in Milton, Massachusetts, said, "In an average winter, we remove eight to ten snowy owls from Logan Airport near Boston. During the 2013–2014 winter, we removed 120."

Some snowies returned to the airport after they were removed and relocated.

PROJECT SNOWSTORM

In December 2013, Norman Smith was excited about the opportunity to study snowy owls. Even owl experts knew very little about snowies' wintertime behavior and migration patterns. So Smith contacted three scientist friends around the Northeast, David Brinker, Scott Weidensaul, and Steve Huy. They all knew this irruption of snowy owls could be the biggest in their lifetimes. They also already had a team of volunteers from a separate owl program that could help with research. Brinker said, "We realized we needed to take advantage of our network of owl banders . . . to collect more data about snowies." They founded Project SNOWstorm to band a large number of the snowy owls that had come south that winter.

Norman Smith releases a snowy named Duxbury after it's been banded.

Banding a bird involves attaching a small band to its leg. The band has an ID number and contact information for the banding organization. Before releasing the bird, researchers record its weight, measurements, and where it was first caught. Then, if that bird is caught again, others can record updated information and report it.

Banding is a common way to gain insights into a bird's physical condition and travels. However, it relies on the bird surviving and being caught again by someone who will both record and report any updates.

Brinker, Weidensaul, and Huy launched Project SNOWstorm during the irruption, aiming to band a large number of snowy owls. They hoped the project would provide more information about where snowies travel during winter migrations.

This is an example of a typical bird band.

Then Weidensaul's friend Andrew McGann heard about Project SNOWstorm. As a biologist interested in birds, he was fascinated by the snowy owl irruption. And McGann saw an opportunity for scientists to take their research to the next level. He suggested, "Why not do more than just band snowies? Why not outfit some with GPS transmitters?"

McGann worked at Cellular Tracking Technologies (CTT), which builds GPS devices to track wildlife. He convinced CTT to custom-build GPS transmitters small enough and light enough for snowy owls to wear.

Snowy owls can turn their heads about 270 degrees—far enough to look behind them.

Project SNOWstorm needed to raise money for the transmitters—each cost $3,000. News of the project spread. After receiving some donations early on from individuals and birding groups, the operation went online, explaining the group's mission on a crowdfunding page that asked people all across the Internet to donate. Soon Project SNOWstorm was able to purchase two dozen of the special GPS units. The tracking project was on!

A crowd gathers to watch Norman Smith release a snowy owl named Century.

TRACKING TECHNOLOGY

Running on a solar-powered battery, the transmitter uses the GPS (Global Positioning System) network of satellites in orbit around Earth to calculate a snowy owl's exact location at the moment it's checked. The device collects this data every thirty minutes, if its battery is charged enough. It also records how high the snowy is flying, what direction it's going, and how fast it's moving. Then it sends that data to CTT computers every three days, if it can access a cell phone network. And CTT shares the data with Project SNOWstorm.

The GPS transmitter that Project SNOWstorm used is only 2.6 inches (6.7 cm) long, 1.5 inches (3.7 cm) wide, and 0.7 inches (1.9 cm) high. It's the perfect size to fit on a snowy's back.

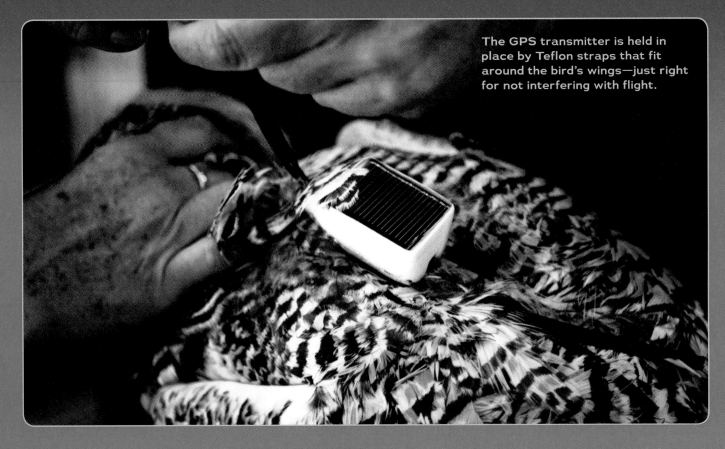

The GPS transmitter is held in place by Teflon straps that fit around the bird's wings—just right for not interfering with flight.

Other transmitters that track animals can transmit by satellite, which allows them to send data from remote areas. But the CTT transmitters send data back to CTT computers through cellular towers, which is a lot faster and cheaper.

However, when the owl flies out of cell phone range, the transmitter can no longer send data. It still stores any data that had already been recorded, though—even if there's not enough sunshine to charge the batteries, such as during the Arctic winter. And the data is stored for as long as five years.

The team of researchers began to outfit snowies with the transmitters in December 2013. They gave each owl an official tracking name related to where it was caught.

The first two Project SNOWstorm owls were Assateague, captured in Maryland on December 17, and Buena Vista, captured in Wisconsin on December 23. When the birds' transmitters started sending data, the researchers gained immediate insights into how different the behavior of wintering snowy owls could be. Buena Vista stayed very close to a marsh area for several weeks. The researchers guessed from his movements that he was finding plenty of food nearby. Assateague, on the other hand, zigzagged along the Atlantic coast.

Two more snowies that were caught in New York, at Cranberry Pond and Braddock Bay, revealed other behavior. Instead of staying on or near land, like Buena Vista and Assateague, these two snowies spent a lot of time away from land, over Lake Ontario. As the researchers studied the owl caught at Cranberry Pond, they could even tell that this snowy spent quite a bit of time just drifting on ice rafts in the lake.

The GPS transmitter weighs only 1.7 ounces (48 g)—slightly more than eight US quarters.

As researchers learned more about wintering snowy owl behavior, they were able to use that information to help snowies.

For example, the Project SNOWstorm results showed that snowies are usually active at night over the winter. Experts previously thought they hunted during the day, because snowies hunt in daylight during the summertime. But in their Arctic home, daylight lasts nearly all day in the summer. Researchers discovered that when snowies had the opportunity to hunt in the dark, when it was easier to avoid being spotted by prey, they took it. So the best time to trap and remove these owls from airports was at night.

While in flight, snowy owls use their keen eyesight and great hearing to help them locate prey.

The Project SNOWstorm results also showed that snowies generally fly faster, higher, and farther than previously thought. So, once captured, snowies needed to be relocated farther away from airports than they were normally being moved. And to encourage them to stay in a new area, the snowies needed plenty of available prey there.

The transmitters did have some problems, though. Sometimes an owl spent too much time in the shade or tugged feathers over the transmitter while preening (cleaning and straightening feathers). Then the solar batteries didn't recharge enough to record much data, or the device recorded data only during brief periods when the batteries did recharge. So the transmitter didn't work properly.

Some snowies migrated out of cell tower range and never came back within range. Those owls may have remained in the Arctic year-round. Or they may not have survived to have a long life.

This snowy perches atop a spotlight near a New York airport runway. Luckily, it's in the sun because as long as the battery in its transmitter is exposed to sunlight at some point, it recharges. Then the battery can keep going for years.

So for most Project SNOWstorm owls, the researchers had only spotty data to study. However, during the following winter, the snowy owl research would get the boost it needed when Project SNOWstorm attached a transmitter to a snowy owl that had been banded the year before.

In the wild, snowies may live ten years or even longer.

A Star Owl Reporter

Two-year-old Baltimore is young, healthy, and ready for duty, transmitting data about his travels.

Baltimore's journey to fame began one day in late January 2015, when David Brinker received a call from the USDA Wildlife Services. They had recovered an owl that Project SNOWstorm had banded the previous winter. It was a snowy named Baltimore. This time, Baltimore was given a transmitter before being released. His transmitter immediately began reporting—and kept on reporting. The data tracking Baltimore poured in until April. Then the snowy owl flew into northern Canada, passing beyond the farthest cell phone towers. No more was heard from Baltimore through the spring, summer, and fall. Until . . .

While Baltimore is resting in the sun, his GPS transmitter is perfectly positioned to recharge its battery.

One day in early December 2015, Baltimore's transmitter checked in, pinging the CTT computer from Quebec, near Lake Evans. He was back!

The oldest data arrived first, tracking Baltimore's flight north the previous spring. Then Baltimore's transmitter began delivering data that tracked his summer migration across the Arctic. Because he traveled a great deal and didn't keep returning to one spot, scientists decided he must not be hunting to feed a mate on a nest. The researchers believed that Baltimore was about three years old and that he hadn't yet begun to mate.

Later data tracked Baltimore's flight back south. His transmitter was still working when he headed north in April 2016, and it checked in again from southern Ontario on December 25, 2016. This round-trip documentation was groundbreaking.

Project SNOWstorm recorded four outstanding sets of snowy owl migration tracks. These are based on the number of GPS locations recorded for each owl: Baltimore (green), 14,597; Erie (yellow), 13,648; Buckeye (red), 10,649; and Braddock (blue), 9,246.

Tracking
Baltimore and
Other Snowy
Owls

NUNAVUT

Hudson
Bay

SASKATCHUAN

MANITOBA

C A N A D A

ONTARIO

QUEBEC

UNITED

STATES

Baltimore

Braddock

Erie

Buckeye

Map based on data
supplied by David Brinker
of Project SNOWStorm

the Future is Snowy

Researchers are watching for more updates from Baltimore so they can keep learning from him. But they also hope to learn more from other Project SNOWstorm owls.

In fact, after about twenty months of silence from Buena Vista's transmitter, in January 2016, it connected to a cell tower in Manitoba, Canada, just north of the North Dakota border. Buena Vista had last transmitted from Wisconsin on March 31, 2014. However, Buena Vista's return to cell phone range was brief. The transmitter sent the oldest data first, reporting data from April 1 through June 7, 2014—then nothing. Did the transmitter quit working? Or did Buena Vista, perhaps, go back to the Arctic to mate?

While the lives of individual snowies such as Buena Vista remain largely unknown, their transmissions have added pieces to the puzzle. Each has helped expand understanding of snowy owl migration.

This is another Project SNOWstorm owl, a male called Amishtown. He was captured at the Pennsylvania Internatonal Airport near Philadelphia, Pennsylvania, in February 2014. He was relocated away from the airport and outfitted with a GPS transmitter before being released.

In addition, researchers are continuing to study the owls' Arctic home region as climate change shifts weather patterns there and around the globe. Snowy owl irruptions are driven by regular lemming boom cycles, but changing weather patterns could mean less frequent lemming cycles. That may result in fewer snowy irruptions and possibly lower snowy owl populations overall.

"Snowy owl irruptions are at risk from climate change," said Weidensaul.

The Arctic is huge, and when the lemming population is booming in one area and not in another, snowies travel to the place with lots of lemmings and raise their chicks there.

No one knows exactly how climate change will affect the Arctic, but researchers are certain it will. According to Weidensaul, in Norway and parts of Greenland, climate change has already altered winter precipitation and snowpack conditions. And, he said, "Lemming [boom] cycles have collapsed—and along with them, the snowy owl populations in those areas."

If the snowy owls' Arctic lemming supply shrinks, they will face greater competition for hunting territories where food is available, just as when the snowy population booms. So researchers wonder if snowy owls might then adapt by migrating south to hunt with less competition during the winter—even traveling into areas near people.

This snowy owl is hunting near New York City.

The irruption of 2013–2014 and the new tracking technology gave researchers a never-before-possible chance to follow the migration routes and wintertime behavior of snowy owls. The more researchers understand about snowies, the better prepared they'll be to protect these birds whenever they migrate into populated areas. This will be key to helping keep snowy owls safe, while they're at rest in an area and while they're on the move.

And as researchers learn, they can teach people everywhere how to be good neighbors to snowy owls—especially when there's a snowy owl invasion.

One way to be a good neighbor to snowy owls is to not disturb them.

AUTHOR'S NOTE

In this story, scientists were tracking snowy owls during and after the historic 2013–2014 irruption. What's not in the story is how I was tracking the scientists.

I have to admit I love the detective work it takes to uncover this kind of scientific story. First, I had to figure out which key people I needed to talk to. What did they do, and what roles did they play in discoveries being made? Next, I had to get in touch with them. For this story, my biggest challenge was contacting Dr. Denver Holt. When I finally talked to him, he was at a remote research site in Alaska on a satellite phone. The reception was terrible until he bundled up and went outside, where it was 24°F (-4.4°C). I imagined the tundra around him and could hear the wind blowing as he talked about his research, answered my questions about what drives irruptions, and shared the possible ways climate change may affect snowy owl breeding behavior.

Like every investigation behind the stories I write, this one grew bigger and bigger. Talking to David Brinker meant I also needed to hear about Project SNOWstorm from Scott Weidensaul, Steve Huy, and Norman Smith. Finding out about the early reports from Newfoundland, Canada, meant tracking down Ken Knowles, who was there and participated in recording those early snowy owl sightings. To understand the technology aspect of the story, I needed to talk to Andrew McGann, who told me how the Cellular Tracking Technologies GPS transmitter was customized especially for snowy owls.

Firsthand is the key word for me when I research and write about this kind of scientific story. Of course, I also researched snowy owls and this irruption through scientific resources and news stories. But I wanted to hear firsthand from the people who lived what happened. That's how I sensed their excitement, learned about the struggles they faced, and heard their awe as they shared what was extraordinary to them. That was what I wanted to carry forward as I brought this story to life.

SOURCE NOTES

5 Ken Knowles, naturalist and birder tour leader, Wildland Tours, interview with the author, July 29, 2016.

5 David Brinker, wildlife biologists and cofounder of Project SNOWstorm, interview with the author, July 21, 2016.

11 Denver Holt, president, Owl Research Institute, interview with the author, June 29, 2016.

13 Ibid.

25 Norman Smith, director, Massachusetts Audubon's Blue Hills Trailside Museum, interview with the author, June 9, 2016.

26 Brinker, interview.

28 Andrew McGann, product specialist, Cellular Tracking Technologies, interview with the author, August 4, 2016.

42 Scott Weidensaul, founding board member of the Ned Smith Center for Nature and Art and cofounder of Project SNOWstorm, interview with the author, August 11, 2016.

43 Weidensaul, interview.

GLOSSARY

ecosystem: a group of interacting living things within the environment where they live

fledge: to develop the wing muscles and feathers needed for flight

Global Positioning System (GPS) transmitter: an electronic device that uses the Global Positioning System network of satellites in Earth orbit to calculate its exact location anywhere on the planet, in degrees latitude and longitude. It then transmits (sends) that position data to a computer. The GPS transmitter also communicates altitude, direction, and traveling speed.

irruption: a sudden migration of a large number of animals to a new area and often far from where they're usually found

migration: seasonal movement of animals from one region to another

predator: an animal that hunts and eats other animals in order to live.

prey: an animal that a predator hunts

rodent: a member of the family of mammals, including mice, rats, and lemmings, with upper and lower pairs of incisor teeth

talon: the claw of a bird, such as a snowy owl, that hunts prey

tundra: a flat area lacking tall trees, in which soil beneath the surface layer is permanently frozen

wingspan: the distance between the wingtips of a flying bird's outstretched wings

FIND OUT MORE

BioKids: Snowy Owl
http://www.biokids.umich.edu/critters/Nyctea_scandiaca/
Check out this page for lots of details about snowy owls, from their size and life cycle to how they communicate to the important role they play in their ecosystem.

Hirsch, Rebecca E. *Thousand-Mile Fliers and Other Amazing Migrators*. Minneapolis: Lerner Publications, 2017.
Find out how the long annual migrations of wildebeests, monarch butterflies, leatherback sea turtles, and arctic terns compare with the snowy owl's lengthy trips to and from the Arctic.

Mass Audubon: Snowy Owl Project
http://www.massaudubon.org/get-outdoors/wildlife-sanctuaries/blue-hills-trailside-museum/snowy-owl-project
Watch a video of a young male snowy owl being released after it was rescued from an airport. This page for the Massachusetts Audubon's Snowy Owls Project also includes information about spotting snowies, snowies at airports, and more.

Nature. "Magic of the Snowy Owl." Preview. YouTube video, 3:19. Posted by "PBS," August 6, 2012. https://www.youtube.com/watch?v=d2c-PHB18fU.
This preview of an episode of *Nature* takes an in-depth look at a family of snowy owls as parents work to raise their chicks in the harsh Arctic environment.

Patrick, Roman. *Snowy Owls*. New York: Gareth Stevens, 2010.
Take a closer look at how snowy owls are adapted for life in the tundra.

Project SNOWstorm
http://www.projectsnowstorm.org/
Follow along with the most up-to-date research from the SNOWstorm team. Blog posts reveal the most recent excitement, and maps show where they're finding new owls to monitor as well as where owls with trackers are traveling.

"Secrets of the Snowy Owl | Field Trip!" YouTube video, 8:42. Posted by "Skunk Bear," May 23, 2016. https://www.youtube.com/watch?v=HXwrB216bgE.
Follow an owl sleuth as he goes on a mission to track down Baltimore, the famous snowy owl, by following his locations throughout the United States and Canada. This video comes from National Public Radio's Skunk Bear YouTube channel, which addresses all sorts of science questions.

INDEX

PHOTO ACKNOWLEDGMENTS

The images in this book are used with the permission of: iStock.com/SeventhDayPhotography, p. 1; iStock.com/Joesboy, p. 4; Nathaniel Grann/The Washington Post/Getty Images, p. 5; John E. Marriott/Getty Images, p. 6; © Daniel J. Cox/NaturalExposures.com, pp. 7, 8, 9 (both), 10, 13, 20, 42; Wayne Lynch/All Canada Photos/Getty Images, p. 12; © Jim Zuckerman/Jaynes Gallery/DanitaDelimont.com/Gallo Images/Getty Images, pp. 14, 21; EVA HAMBACH/AFP/Getty Images, p. 15; © Sergey Gorshkov/Minden Pictures, p. 16; iStock.com/SeventhDayPhotography, p. 17; © Laura Westlund/Independent Picture Service, pp. 18, 39; Roberta Olenick/All Canada Photos/Getty Images, p. 19; © Jim Verhagen, pp. 22, 37; Jim Cumming/Moment RF/Getty Images, p. 23; © Connor Stefanison/Minden Pictures, p. 24; © Ray MacDonald, pp. 26, 29, 30, 32; Oliver Edwards/Mint Images RF/Getty Images, p. 27; © Donald M. Jones/Minden Pictures, p. 28; © National Public Radio, p. 31; Ghost Bear/Shutterstock.com, p. 33; John Cancalosi/Photolibrary/Getty Images, p. 34; Vicki Jauron, Babylon and Beyond Photography/Moment/Getty Images, p. 35; © Chris Hudson, p. 36; © Photograph by Alan Richard, p. 40; © FrancoisPortmann/fotoportmann, p. 43; iStock.com/stanley45, p. 44.

Front cover: Brian Kushner/Alamy Stock Photo.